中华人民共和国文化和旅游部

2023年文化和旅游发展统计公报

STATISTICAL COMMUNIQUÉ OF THE MINISTRY OF CULTURE AND TOURISM OF THE PEOPLE'S REPUBLIC OF CHINA ON CULTURAL AND TOURISM DEVELOPMENT IN 2023

中华人民共和国文化和旅游部 编

中国统计出版社
China Statistics Press

图书在版编目（CIP）数据

中华人民共和国文化和旅游部2023年文化和旅游发展统计公报 = Statistical Communiqué of the Ministry of Culture and Tourism of the People's Republic of China on Cultural and Tourism Development in 2023 ：汉、英 / 中华人民共和国文化和旅游部编 . 北京 ：中国统计出版社，2024. 9. -- ISBN 978-7-5230-0533-0

Ⅰ. G12；F592

中国国家版本馆 CIP 数据核字第 2024C3S101 号

中华人民共和国文化和旅游部2023年文化和旅游发展统计公报

作　　者／中华人民共和国文化和旅游部
责任编辑／张　怡
出版发行／中国统计出版社有限公司
通信地址／北京市丰台区西三环南路甲6号　邮政编码／100073
电　　话／邮购（010）63376909　书店（010）68783171
网　　址／http://www.zgtjcbs.com/
印　　刷／天津画中画印刷有限公司
经　　销／新华书店
开　　本／880mm×1230mm　1/16
字　　数／50千字
印　　张／2.25
版　　别／2024年9月第1版
版　　次／2024年9月第1次印刷
定　　价／28.00元　28.00yuan(RMB)

目录

CONTENTS

中华人民共和国文化和旅游部 2023 年文化和旅游发展统计公报[1]

2023 年，在以习近平同志为核心的党中央坚强领导下，全国文化和旅游系统坚持以习近平新时代中国特色社会主义思想为指导，认真贯彻落实党的二十大精神，深入学习贯彻习近平文化思想，坚持稳中求进工作总基调，完整、准确、全面贯彻新发展理念，着力推动高质量发展，统筹好发展和安全，坚持以社会主义核心价值观为引领，以满足人民文化需求和增强人民精神力量为着力点，努力创作优秀文化作品、提供优秀文化产品和优质旅游产品，推动文化和旅游行业实现快速恢复发展，有力发挥了稳定增长、促进消费、扩大就业、惠及民生的重要作用。

2023 年末，纳入统计报送的全国各类文化和旅游单位[2]30.4 万个。其中，各级文化和旅游部门所属单位 6.6 万个，从业人员[3]72.9 万人。

一、艺术创作生产持续繁荣

2023 年，文化和旅游部实施 2023—2025 舞台艺术、美术创作行动计划以及中国民族歌剧传承发展工程等新时代系列艺术创作工程，推出一批优秀作品。组织《掀起你的盖头来—新疆是个好地方》全国巡演，“文艺中国”新春特别节目、陕北民歌音乐会全国巡演以及新时代舞台艺术优秀剧目展演、中国歌剧节、戏曲百戏（昆山）盛典、全国优秀儿童戏剧展演、全国地方戏精粹展演、国家艺术院团演出演播季、中国设计大展及公共艺术专题展等 30 余项艺术活动。举办第十届中国京剧艺术节，共组织 24 台京剧优秀剧目展演、4 台文化和旅游部全国戏曲表演领军人才培养计划京剧专场演出、5 台京剧艺术表演人才提升计划汇报演出、4 台川剧精品剧目展演、18 场折子戏公益演出。

2023 年末，全国共有艺术表演团体[4]1.8 万个，从业人员 38.5 万人。全年共演出 254.2 万场，国内观众 9.0 亿人次，演出收入 207.8 亿元。全年原创首演剧目 1993 部，原创首演节目 3805 个。

2023 年末，全国共有艺术表演场馆 3060 个，观众座席数 213.6 万个。全年艺术表演场馆共演出

41.5 万场，观众 12273.4 万人次。

2023 年末，全国共有公共美术馆[5]707 个，从业人员 0.6 万人。全年共举办展览 9813 场，同比增长 36.5%，参观人次 6217.9 万，同比增长 86.4%。

二、公共服务体系不断健全

2023 年，文化和旅游部加快推进现代公共文化服务体系建设，提升乡镇综合文化站服务效能，推动新型公共文化空间建设。推进全国智慧图书馆体系和公共文化云项目建设。进一步推动落实基本公共文化服务标准。开展第七次全国县级以上公共图书馆评估定级工作，共评定一级公共图书馆 1302 家、二级公共图书馆 680 家、三级公共图书馆 741 家。开展公共图书馆、文化馆服务宣传周活动。推进国家公共文化服务体系示范区创新发展。实施“春雨工程”——文化和旅游志愿服务边疆行计划，指导东中部地区与边疆民族地区文化和旅游机构达成 364 个结对合作项目。打造“四季村晚”“大地欢歌”“大地情深”、广场舞大会等群众文化活动品牌。

1. 公共图书馆

2023 年末，全国共有公共图书馆[6]3246 个，从业人员 6.1 万人。其中，具有高级职称人员 0.8 万人，占 13.0%；具有中级职称人员 1.9 万人，占 31.2%。

2023 年末，全国公共图书馆实际使用房屋建筑面积 2259.6 万平方米，同比增长 7.7%；全国图书总藏量[7]14.4 亿册，同比增长 5.6%；阅览室座席数 168.0 万个，同比增长 8.3%。

2023 年末，全国平均每万人公共图书馆建筑面积 160.3 平方米，比上年末增加 11.7 平方米，全国人均图书藏量 1.02 册，比上年末增加 0.06 册；全年全国人均购书费 1.6 元，与上年基本持平。

图 1 2013-2023 年全国公共图书馆人均资源情况

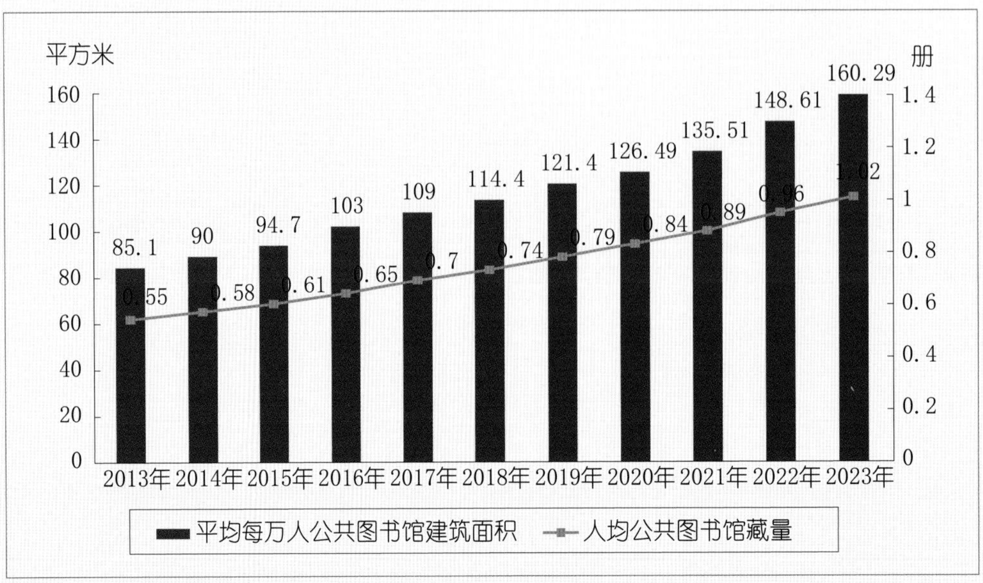

全年公共图书馆总流通人次[8]116061 万人次，同比增长 46.9%；书刊文献外借 78299 万册次，同比增长 29.0%；外借人次 33044 万人次，同比增长 32.7%。全年共为读者举办各种活动 293504 次，同比增长 38.3%；参加人次 21380 万，同比增长 58.4%。

图 2 2013-2023 年全国公共图书馆总流通人次及书刊外借册次

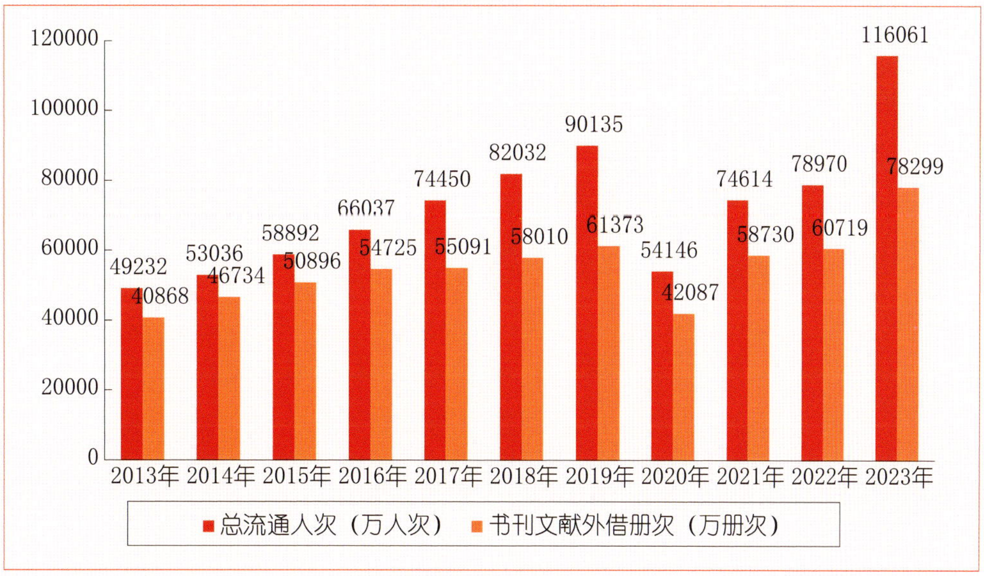

2. 群众文化机构

2023 年末，全国共有群众文化机构[9]4.4 万个，从业人员 19.9 万人。其中，具有高级职称的人员 0.8 万人，占 4.0%；具有中级职称人员 1.8 万人，占 9.4%。

图 3 2013-2023 年全国平均每万人群众文化设施建筑面积

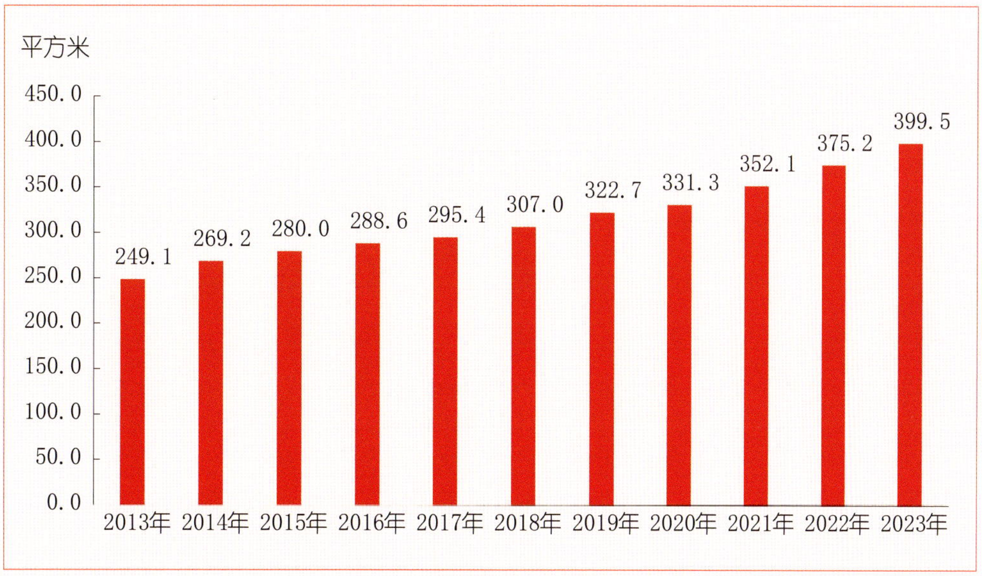

2023 年末，全国群众文化机构实际使用房屋建筑面积 5631.6 万平方米，同比增长 7.8%。年末全国平均每万人群众文化设施建筑面积 399.5 平方米，同比增长 6.5%。

全年全国群众文化机构共组织开展各类文化活动[10]412 万场，同比增长 53.5%；服务人次 183537 万人次，同比增长 91.6%。

2023 年末，全国群众文化机构共有馆办文艺团体[11]9843 个，全年演出 14.9 万场，观众 10651.7 万人次。

表 1 2023 年全国群众文化机构活动开展情况

项　目	总量		比上年增长（%）	
	活动次数（万场次）	服务人次（万人次）	活动次数	服务人次
各项活动总计	**412**	**183537**	**53.5**	**91.6**
其中：文艺活动	246	139298	54.0	103.7
训练班	135	10462	55.6	54.4
展览	25	32673	41.9	64.5
公益性讲座	6	1104	41.8	44.8

三、文化遗产保护传承有力推进

1. 文物保护利用。2023 年，文化和旅游部、国家文物局持续推进中华文明探源工程和“考古中国”重大项目。水下考古取得重大突破，深海考古迈向世界先进水平，边疆考古不断加强。启动第四次全国文物普查，强化国家考古遗址公园保护建设，加强大运河、长江文物保护利用，实施廊桥、壁画彩塑、东北抗联革命文物保护计划，深入推进革命文物保护利用工程，保护利用水平持续提高。普洱景迈山古茶林文化景观成功申遗。加大对文物违法案件督察约谈、查处追责力度，持续开展打击防范文物犯罪专项行动。印发《关于加强文物科技创新的意见》，举办全国文物行业职业技能大赛等，文物科技创新和人才培养持续加强。加强国家文物保护利用示范区创建管理，深化革命文物主题陈列展览展示。开展国际博物馆日、“文化和自然遗产日”文物展示传播活动，联合摄制《寻古中国》《何以中国》，文物传播影响力持续提升。三星堆博物馆新馆、浙江省博物馆之江馆等新馆建成开放，举办“鉴往知远——新时代考古成果展”等精品大展，带动“博物馆热”持续升温。文物国际交流合作深化拓展，牵头成立亚洲文化遗产保护联盟。实施中华古籍保护计划、古籍保护人才培育计划，出台古籍类文物定级工作指南，加强水书、甲骨文保护，组织全国古籍重点保护单位复核抽查，推进古籍数字化整理、中华古籍智慧化服务平台建设，古籍保护利用更加科学规范。

2023 年末，全国共有各类文物机构 9645 个，从业人员 18.1 万人，其中高级职称 1.3 万人，占

7.0%；中级职称 2.4 万人，占 13.1%。全国登记备案博物馆、纪念馆达到 6833 个。

2023 年末，全国文物机构藏品 5017.2 万件／套，其中，文物系统管理的国有博物馆藏品 3363.3 万件／套，占藏品总量的 67.0%。

2023 年，全国各类文物机构共举办陈列展览 3.0 万个，其中，基本陈列[12]1.3 万个，临时展览[13]1.7 万个。接待观众 140266 万人次，同比增长 119.3%，其中未成年人 32203 万人次，同比增长 101.2%，占参观总人数的 23.0%。文物系统管理的国有博物馆接待观众 102129 万人次，同比增长 123.7%，占文物机构接待观众总数的 72.8%。

图 4 2013-2023 年全国文物机构接待观众人次及未成年人观众人次

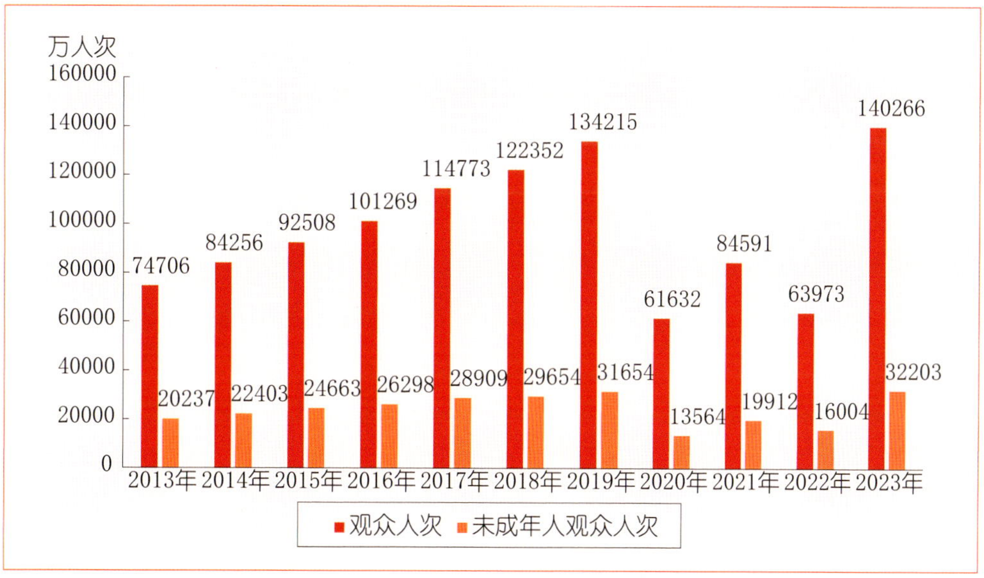

2. 非物质文化遗产保护传承。2023 年，文化和旅游部扎实推进第六批国家级非遗代表性传承人认定工作，继续壮大非遗代表性传承人队伍。实施黄河流域、大运河非遗保护行动计划，开展传统工艺项目存续状况评估。推进非遗助力乡村振兴，截至目前，各地共建设 6700 余家非遗工坊。实施中国非遗传承人研修培训计划，调整公布新一批 130 所参与培训院校名单。公布 10 个国家级文化生态保护区、公示 100 家国家级非遗生产性保护示范基地。推动非遗与旅游深度融合发展。举办中国成都国际非遗节、中国原生民歌节、非遗品牌大会、非遗购物节、“文化进万家——视频直播家乡年”等活动。组织春节非遗传承实践相关活动 1.2 万余场、“文化和自然遗产日”非遗宣传展示活动 9800 余场。摄制播出《非遗里的中国》，收看及互动人次超过 75.4 亿，非遗传播力度持续扩大。

截至 2023 年末，共有国家级非遗代表性项目 1557 项，共有在世国家级非遗代表性传承人 2241 名。列入联合国教科文组织非遗名录、名册项目 43 个。

全国共有非物质文化遗产保护机构 2406 个，从业人员 1.7 万人。全年全国各类非物质文化遗产保护机构举办演出8.2万场，同比增长41.5%；举办民俗活动1.8万场，同比增长30.4%；举办展览2.2万场，同比增长20.1%。

四、市场发展和管理能力有效提升

2023年，文化和旅游部积极推动文化和旅游领域稳增长、助企纾困帮扶政策延续实施。推进文化和旅游市场电子证照应用，开发“文旅市场通”APP，推进“一网通办”。加强大型营业性演出活动规范管理。强化脱口秀演出、卡拉OK音乐曲目内容管理。推进文化和旅游市场信用体系建设，开展文明旅游宣传引导、文化和旅游市场信用经济发展试点。组织举办全国星级饭店从业人员服务技能竞赛和全国导游大赛，不断提升行业发展能力。

2023年，指导31个省（区、市）出台省级文化市场综合执法事项指导目录。加强大型营业性演出执法监管，指导各地建立完善大型营业性演出执法监管长效机制。开展营业性演出票务专项整治行动，严厉查处演出票务市场违法违规行为。持续开展旅游市场秩序整治，依法查处未经许可经营旅行社业务、“不合理低价游”等违法违规行为。会同中宣部版权局印发《关于进一步加强青少年版权保护工作的通知》，深入推进未成年人保护工作。持续深化全国文化市场技术监管与服务平台建设与应用，升级优化平台综合执法系统。加强网络动态监测，处理问题线索9.7万条。处置举报投诉信息3.9万条。

2023年末，全国通过统计直报系统报送和审核的文化市场经营单位[14]17.5万家，从业人员117.7万人，营业收入17852.5亿元，营业利润1387.1亿元。其中，娱乐场所4.5万个，从业人员41.8万人，营业收入589.6亿元，营业利润39.5亿元。互联网上网服务营业场所9.0万个，从业人员14.7万人，营业收入181.8亿元。演出市场单位2.4万个，从业人员42.3万人，营业收入7057.8亿元，营业利润283.9亿元。艺术品经营机构0.7万个，从业人员2.2万人，营业收入563.8亿元，营业利润137.8亿元。经营性互联网文化单位0.8万家，从业人员16.7万人，营业收入9459.5亿元，营业利润877.7亿元。

五、文化产业和科技发展不断深化

2023年，文化和旅游部继续组织开展文化和旅游消费促进活动，实施“百城百区”金融支持文化和旅游消费行动计划。印发《国家级夜间文化和旅游消费集聚区建设指引》。推动国家文化和旅游消费示范城市及试点城市、国家级夜间文化和旅游消费集聚区建设。开展文化产业赋能乡村振兴试点工作，公布首批63个文化产业赋能乡村振兴试点名单。推进区域文化产业带建设，加强国家级文化产业示范园区（基地）规范管理。组织举办“多彩中国 佳节好物”文化和旅游贸易促进活动。出台金融支持乡村旅游高质量发展、提升暑期旅游景区开放管理水平政策措施。举办全国文化和旅游项目建设暨投融资大会，分别与中国进出口银行、中国农业银行签署战略合作协议。完善文化和旅游部产业项目协调推进机制，推动落实文化和旅游领域设备更新贷款贴息政策。公布首批 2 个国家文化与金融合作示范区。推动文化和旅游基础设施 REITs 应用，推动旅游业纳入政府和社会资本合作新机制。公布 50 家国家文化产业和旅游产业融合发展示范区建设单位。实施国有文艺院团数字演艺"一团一品"培育开发项目，发布全国旅游演艺精品名录，组织举办全国演艺博览会。

据国家统计局统计，2023 年全国规模以上文化及相关产业企业实现营业收入 129515 亿元，同比增长 8.2%。

2023 年，文化和旅游部持续推进实施国家文化数字化战略，与国家网信办共同举办第六届数字中国建设峰会数字文化分论坛，发布 2023 年文化和旅游数字化创新示范案例 44 个。加强科技创新驱动，推荐立项国家重点研发项目 2 个，发布文化和旅游创新研发项目和部重点实验室项目 18 项，新认定 8 家旅游科技示范园区，建设 12 个文化和旅游部技术创新中心。印发《文化和旅游标准化工作管理办法》，进一步规范文化和旅游标准化工作，推动出台国家标准 5 项，批准发布行业标准 15 项、立项 28 项，推进 2 项国际标准立项，覆盖旅游、剧场、图书馆、文化馆、非遗、网络文化、动漫等领域，涉及乡村旅游、智慧旅游等业态评价，旅游景区、饭店、演艺新空间、网络表演等管理服务要求，演出设备、动漫平台等技术规范，不断提升管理和服务水平，为行业高质量发展奠定了基础。推进中国艺术学"三大体系"建设，立项国家社科基金艺术学项目 251 个、部级研究项目 53 个、青年科研人才扶持计划项目 42 个。牵头推进研学旅游规范发展，研究起草指导性文件。实施全国文化艺术和旅游职业教育提质培优行动计划项目 39 项。

六、旅游业发展稳步向好

2023 年，文化和旅游部贯彻落实《关于释放旅游消费潜力推动旅游业高质量发展的若干措施》，印发《国内旅游提升计划（2023—2025 年）》，进一步释放旅游消费潜力，推动旅游业高质量发展。印发《东北地区旅游业发展规划》，推进长江、黄河文化保护传承规划、大运河文化和旅游融合发展规划落地实施。积极参与长江经济带发展、京津冀协同发展、中部地区崛起、东北全面振兴等政策规划制定。编制《长江国家文化公园建设保护规划》，助力打造中华文化重要标识，加强长城国家文化公园重点段建设。实施旅游促进各民族交往交流交融计划，助力铸牢中华民族共同体意识。新评定国家级旅游度假区 18 家、旅游休闲街区 110 家、滑雪旅游度假地 7 家以及国家体育旅游示范基地 13 家、工业旅游示范基地 69 家。推出首批全国智慧旅游沉浸式体验新空间培育试点名单、"5G+智慧旅游"应用试点项目。推动乡村旅游提质发展，发布"乡村四时好风光"等精品线路。推动实施"用好红色资源 培育时代新人"红色旅游助推铸魂育人行动计划，举办第四届全国红色故事讲解员大赛和第十四届全国大学生红色旅游创意策划大赛。开展"旅游中国 · 美好生活"全国旅游宣传、

“全国欢乐冰雪旅游季”推广活动，举办中国义乌文化和旅游产品交易博览会、中国（武汉）文化旅游博览会、中国旅游产业博览会等，进一步加大对各地文旅产业的宣传推广力度。

2023 年末，全国共有旅行社 56275 家。根据旅行社填报系统数据显示，全年全国旅行社营业收入 4442.7 亿元，营业利润 37.4 亿元。

2023 年末，全国共有 8253 家星级饭店。根据全国旅游监管服务平台数据显示，全年星级饭店营业收入 1609.0 亿元，平均房价 370.8 元 / 间夜，平均出租率 50.7%。

2023 年末，全国共有 A 级景区 15721 个，直接从业人员 160.7 万人。全年接待游客 57.5 亿人次，实现旅游收入 4068.7 亿元。

2023 年，国内出游人次 48.9 亿，同比增长 93.3%。其中，城镇居民国内出游 37.6 亿人次，同比增长 94.9%；农村居民国内出游 11.3 亿人次，同比增长 88.5%。国内游客出游总花费 4.9 万亿元，同比增长 140.3%。其中，城镇居民出游花费 4.2 万亿元，同比增长 147.5%；农村居民出游花费 0.7 万亿元，同比增长 106.4%。

图 5 2013-2023 年国内旅游发展情况

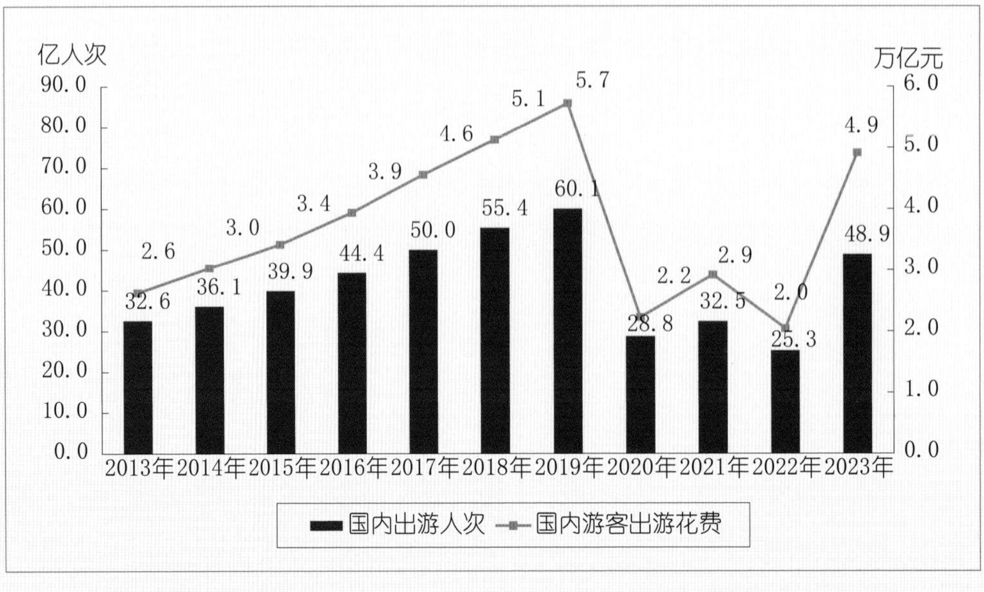

2023 年，入境游客 8203 万人次，其中，外国人 1378 万人次，香港、澳门和台湾同胞 6824 万人次。内地居民出境旅游 8763 万人次。

七、文化和旅游对外和对港澳台交流深度拓展

2023 年，文化和旅游部实施入境旅游促进计划。牵头举办中国—中亚峰会、第三届“一带一路”国际合作高峰论坛文艺演出，成功举办中国西班牙文化和旅游年、“艺汇丝路—采风作品展”暨中阿艺术家对话沙龙、《唐诗的回响》音乐会、纪念费城交响乐团访华 50 周年音乐会等活动，品牌活

动影响力持续提升。开展“你好！中国”国家旅游形象系列推广活动。实施“文化丝路”计划，完善丝绸之路联盟机制。举办“欢乐春节”、“茶和天下”·雅集、“天涯共此时——中秋节”全球联动、“中国故事”讲座、“发现中国之美”、中国国际旅游交易会、丝绸之路（敦煌）国际文化博览会等系列活动，成立丝绸之路旅游城市联盟，提升中华文化传播力影响力。加强中国文化中心、旅游办事处等海外阵地建设。持续深化对港澳台交流交融。举办港澳青少年内地游学联盟大会，有效促进内地与港澳青少年广泛交往和深度交流。促进澳门以中华文化为主流、多元文化共存的交流合作基地建设。举办海峡两岸旅行商大会，为两岸旅游进一步深化合作交流提供了广阔空间。

截至 2023 年末，在全球设有 48 家海外中国文化中心、20 家驻外旅游办事处。此外，在香港设有亚洲旅游交流中心，在台湾设有海峡两岸旅游交流协会台北办事处、高雄办事分处。

八、财政资金保障水平有新的提升

2023 年，全国文化和旅游事业费[15]1280.4 亿元，比上年增加 78.6 亿元，同比增长 6.5%；全国人均文化和旅游事业费 90.8 元，比上年增加 5.7 元，同比增长 6.7%。文化和旅游事业费占财政总支出的比重为 0.47%，比上年提高 0.01 个百分点。

图 6 2013-2023 年人均文化和旅游事业费及增速情况

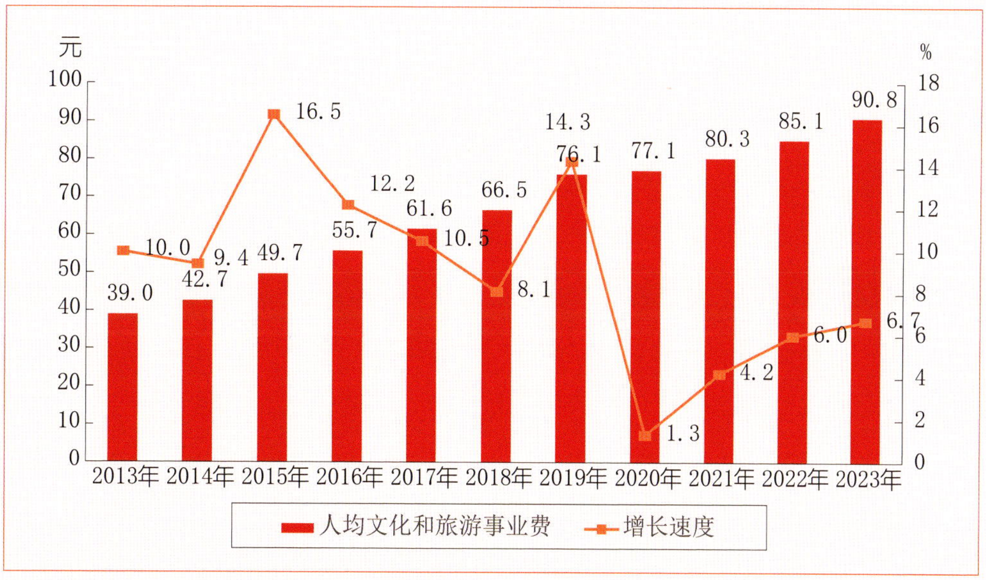

全国文化和旅游事业费中，县以上文化和旅游事业费 597.6 亿元，占 46.7%，比重比上年提升了 1.5 个百分点；县及县以下文化和旅游事业费 682.7 亿元，占 53.3%，比重比上年下降了 1.5 个百分点。东部地区[16]文化和旅游事业费 560.0 亿元，占 43.7%，比重比上年下降了 1.4 个百分点。中部地区文化和旅游事业费 324.1 亿元，占 25.3%，比重比上年提高了 0.1 个百分点。西部地区文化和旅游事业费 367.4 亿元，占 28.7%，比重比上年提高了 1.4 个百分点。

表 2 全国文化和旅游事业费按城乡和区域分布情况

项目		2000	2005	2010	2015	2020	2022	2023
总量（亿元）	全国	63.2	133.8	323.1	686.0	1088.3	1201.8	1280.4
	# 县以上	46.3	98.1	206.7	352.8	501.0	544.3	597.6
	县及县以下	16.9	35.7	116.4	330.1	587.3	658.6	682.7
	# 东部地区	28.9	64.4	143.4	287.9	491.6	542.5	560.0
	中部地区	15.1	30.6	78.7	164.3	269.8	302.6	324.1
	西部地区	13.7	27.6	85.8	193.9	301.6	328.1	367.4
所占比重（%）	全国	100.0	100.0	100.0	100.0	100.0	100.0	100.0
	# 县以上	73.4	73.3	64.0	51.7	46.0	45.2	46.7
	县及县以下	26.7	26.7	36.0	48.3	54.0	54.8	53.3
	# 东部地区	45.7	48.1	44.4	42.1	45.1	45.1	43.7
	中部地区	23.8	22.9	24.3	24.1	24.8	25.2	25.3
	西部地区	21.7	20.6	26.6	28.4	27.7	27.3	28.7

注释：

[1] 本公报中各项数据为初步统计数据。各项统计数据均未包括香港特别行政区、澳门特别行政区和台湾省。部分数据因四舍五入的原因，存在着与分项合计不等的情况。

[2] 文化和旅游单位是指全国各级文化和旅游部门主办的或实行行业管理的文化机构，不含各级新闻出版、广播影视等部门门主办或管理的机构。根据现行的统计制度，各级文化和旅游部门主办单位（如公共图书馆、文化馆、文化站、博物馆、公有制艺术表演团体、公有制艺术表演场馆等）全部纳入统计范围，实行行业管理的文化和旅游单位中，包括娱乐场所和互联网上网服务营业场所、非公有制艺术表演团体、非公有制艺术表演场馆、经营性互联网文化单位、艺术品经营机构和演出经纪机构和 A 级景区、星级饭店和旅行社数据。

[3] 从业人员是指各级文化和旅游部门主办或实行行业管理的机构中工作并取得劳动报酬的人员。

[4] 艺术表演团体指由文化和旅游部门主办或实行行业管理（经文化和旅游行政部门审批并领取营业性演出许可证），专门从事表演艺术等活动的各类专业艺术表演团体，含民间职业剧团。（不包括群众业余文艺表演团队）

[5] 美术馆是指由文化和旅游部门主办或实行行业管理的，具备展览、典藏、研究及公共教育和服务功能的、向公众开放的国有美术馆；以及在民政部门登记注册并在文化和旅游部门备案的，具

备展览、典藏、研究及公共教育和服务功能的、向公众开放的、非营利性的民营美术馆。

[6] 公共图书馆是指文化和旅游部门主办的面向社会服务的图书馆。

[7] 公共图书馆总藏量指本馆已编目的古籍、图书、期刊和报纸的合订本、小册子、手稿，以及缩微制品、录像带、录音带、光盘等视听文献资料数量之和。

[8] 公共图书馆总流通人次是指本年度内到图书馆场馆接受图书馆服务的总人次，包括借阅书刊、咨询问题，以及参加各类读者活动等。

[9] 群众文化机构是指各级文化和旅游部门主办的开展群众文化活动的场所，主要包括文化馆（含综合性文化中心、群众艺术馆）、文化站。

[10] 群众文化机构组织开展活动是指组织文艺活动、举办训练班、举办展览和组织公益性讲座总和。

[11] 群众文化机构馆办文艺团体指由本馆人员组成的为群众提供文艺演出的演出团队。

[12] 基本陈列指在本馆布置陈列、地点固定、时间较长的展出。

[13] 临时展览指在本机构内设置，由本馆设计布陈，形式比较多样的展出。

[14] 文化市场经营单位指经审批或备案并领取相关许可或备案文件的、从事文化经营和文化服务活动的机构。按照现行统计制度，文化市场经营单位统计范围包括娱乐场所和互联网上网服务营业场所、非公有制艺术表演团体、非公有制艺术表演场馆、经营性互联网文化单位、艺术品经营机构和演出经纪机构。

[15] 文化和旅游事业费是指区域内各级财政对文化和旅游系统主办单位的经费投入总和。根据现行统计口径，文化和旅游事业费不包括各级文化和旅游行政部门的行政运行经费。

[16] 东部地区包括北京、天津、辽宁、上海、江苏、浙江、福建、山东、广东；中部地区包括河北、山西、吉林、黑龙江、安徽、江西、河南、湖北、湖南、海南；西部地区包括内蒙古、广西、重庆、四川、贵州、云南、西藏、陕西、甘肃、青海、宁夏、新疆。

Statistical Communiqué of the Ministry of Culture and Tourism of the People's Republic of China on Cultural and Tourism Development in 2023[1]

In 2023, under the firm leadership of the Central Committee of the Communist Party of China with Comrade Xi Jinping at its core, China's cultural and tourism administrations, guided by Xi Jinping Thought on Socialism with Chinese Characteristics for A New Era, implemented the guiding principles from the Party's 20th National Congress, gained a good understanding of Xi Jinping Thought on Culture and acted on it, as well as on the general principle of pursuing progress while ensuring stability, fully and faithfully applying the new development philosophy on all fronts and move faster to create a new pattern of development. Our focus has been unwavering in promoting high-quality growth, all the while ensuring both development and security. Adhering to core socialist values, our endeavors are centered on fulfilling the meet the intellectual and cultural needs of our people.

In pursuit of such a goal, we have dedicated ourselves to supporting the creation of outstanding cultural works and providing high quality cultural and tourism products. These efforts have catalyzed a robust recovery and dynamic growth within the cultural and tourism sectors, which was instrumental in promoting steady economic growth and consumer spending as well as creating more jobs for the benefit of our people.

304,000 national cultural and tourism units[2] were brought into the statistical range by the end of 2023. Among them, 66,000 were affiliated to cultural and tourism authorities at different levels, which hired 729,000 employees[3].

I. A vibrant arts scene

In 2023, the Ministry of Culture and Tourism launched the 2023-2025 Performing Arts and fine arts creation action plan, as well as the Chinese national opera heritage and development project, among a suite of new-era-themed art projects. This resulted in the unveiling of a significant number of high-quality works across various art forms. A diverse array of over 30 cultural activities were organized, including the national tour of "Discover the Beauty of Xinjiang," the "Art China" Chinese New Year special program, a national tour of northern Shaanxi folk music concerts, presentation of outstanding performing arts productions of the new era, Chinese Opera Festival, the xiqu gala (Kunshan), national showcases of outstanding children's theater, a presentation of the best of local folk opera plays, performing season of China’s top national art troupes, and major exhibitions of design and public art. The 10th China Peking Opera Festival was also held, featuring 24 performances of distinguished Peking opera productions, 4 special showcases of Peking opera by leading performers cultivated under the Ministry's national talent development program, 5 performances highlighting Peking opera artists with special advanced training, 4 performances of outstanding Sichuan opera plays, and 18 non-profit shows of selected opera scenes.

By the end of the year, the number of art performance troupes[4] reached 18,000, and the number of professionals reached 385,000. All arts troupes in China presented 2.542 million performances, and the domestic audiences reached 900 million. The total performing arts box office was 20.78 billion yuan. Among all shows, 1,993 theatre productions and 3,805 programs made their debut. By the end of the year, the number of venues of the performing arts amounted to 3,060, with 2,136,000 seats. 415,000 art performances were held throughout the year, and the audience attendance reached 122.734 million.

By the end of 2023, there were 707 art museums[5] in China with 6,000 employees. 9,813 exhibitions were presented by these museums year-round, up by 36.5%, attracting 62.179 million visitor attendances, up by 86.4% over the number of the previous year.

II. An increasingly improved public service system

In 2023, the Ministry of Culture and Tourism accelerated its efforts to modernize the public cultural service system, enhanced the efficiency of cultural stations in townships and drove ahead the development of innovative public cultural spaces. The Ministry advanced the development of a nationwide smart library system and the project of building cloud cultural database for public use, and furthered the implementation of standards for basic public cultural services. The seventh national evaluation and accreditation of public libraries at the county level and above was conducted, crediting 1,302 first-grade, 680 second-grade, and 741 third-grade public libraries. A week-long campaign was organized to spotlight the services provided by public libraries and cultural centers. The Ministry also continued to foster development of model zones of the national public cultural service system. The "Spring Rain Project", a cultural and tourism volunteer service initiative tailored to border regions was implemented, and 364 cooperative projects between cultural and tourism institutions in the east and central regions and their counterparts in border areas were conducted under the Ministry guidance. Moreover, the Ministry launched a series of community cultural activities, including the all-year-long village gala series, vocal artists talent shows, tour of excellent amateur art performances, and public square dance galas.

(1) Public Libraries

By the end of the year, there were in total 3,246 public libraries[6] nationwide, with 61,000 employees. Among them, 8,000 owned senior professional titles, accounting for 13.0%, and 19,000 owned medium-level professional titles, accounting for 31.2%.

According to statistics at the end of 2023, the actual floor space used by public library buildings totaled 225.96 million square meters, up by 7.7% over the end of the previous year. 1.44 billion books were collected[7] in these libraries, up by 5.6%. The number of seats in reading rooms was 1.68 million, up by 8.3%.

By the end of the 2023, the floor space of public libraries for each ten thousand persons was 160.3 square meters, an increase of 11.7 square meters over the end of the previous year; the number of books per capita was 1.02, an increase of 0.06 over the previous year; the money spent on books per capita was 1.6 yuan, basically the same with that of the previous year.

Figure 1: Information of per capita resource of national public libraries in 2013-2023

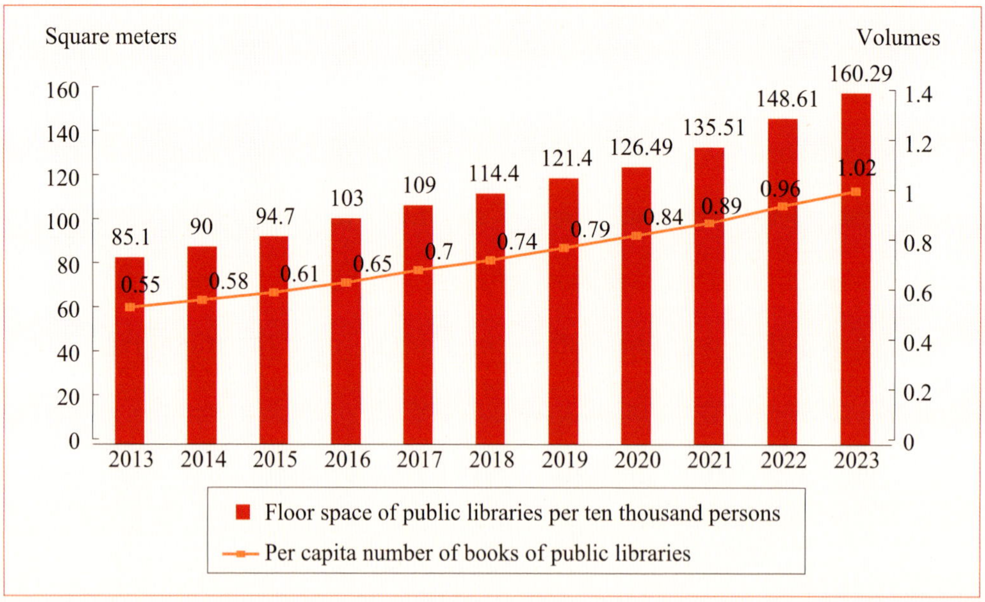

In 2023, the total number of visits[8] made by the people to public libraries reached 116,061 million visits, an increase of 46.9%. The total circulation number of books, magazines, and documents loaned to readers reached 78,299 million copies, up by 29.0%; readers borrowed books for a total of 33,044 million times, an increase of 32.7% over the previous year. The number of various activities organized for readers totaled 293,504, up by 38.3%, which attracted 213.80 million attendances, an increase of 58.4%.

(2) Public and community cultural institutions

There were a total of 44,000 public and community cultural institutions[9] across the country by the end of 2023 and the total employees of public and community cultural institutions nationwide reached 199,000. Staff with senior professional titles reached 8,000, accounting for 4.0%; and staffs with medium-grade professional titles reached 18,000, accounting for 9.4%.

By the end of the year, the actual floor space used by public and community cultural institutions was 56,316,000 square meters, up by 7.8% since the previous year. By the end of the year, the area covered by cultural facilities for every 10,000 people reached 399.5 square meters, an increase of 6.5% since the previous year.

Figure 2: Total flow of person-time and number of books lent out of national public libraries in 2013-2023

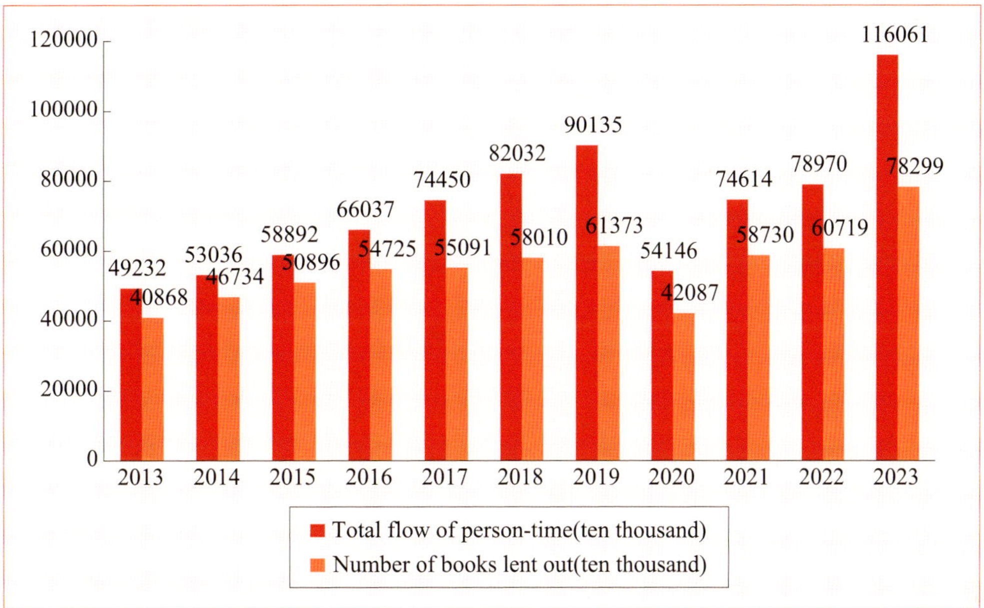

Figure 3: Area of structure of national cultural facilities of mass per ten thousand people in 2013-2023

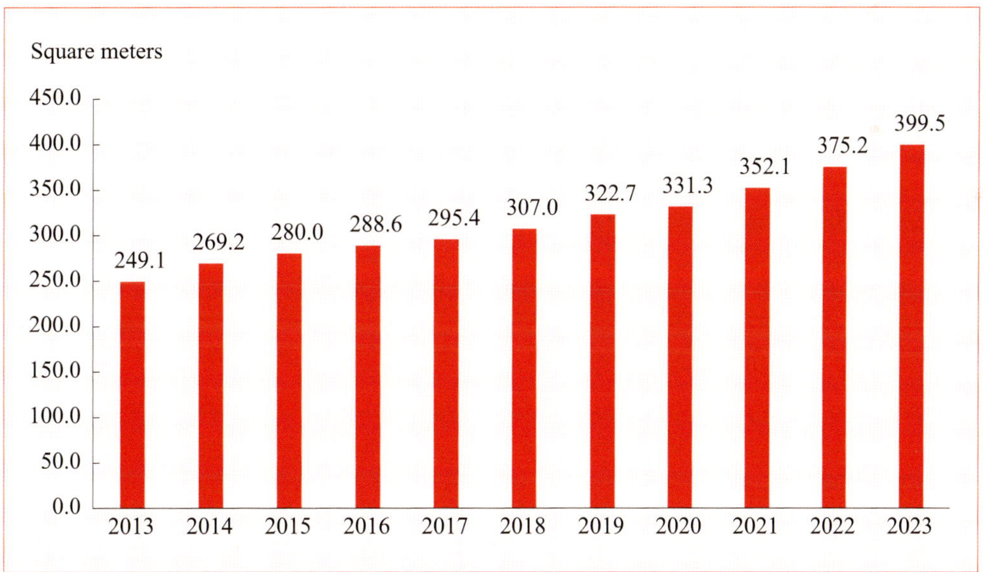

The number of cultural activities[10] organized by nationwide public and community cultural institutions throughout the year reached 4.12 million, up by 53.5% since the previous year; they had 183,537 million views, up by 91.6%.

By the end of the year, public and community cultural institutions nationwide fostered a total of 9,843 cultural and arts groups[11] under cultural centers, which presented 149,000 performances to a total audience of 106,517,000.

Table 1: Information of activities organized by nationwide public and community cultural institutions in 2023

	Gross		Increase over previous year (%)	
	Number of activity (ten thousand shows)	Number of participants (ten thousand person-time)	Number of activity	Person-time of participants
Aggregate of activities	**412**	**183537**	**53.5**	**91.6**
#Art Performances	246	139298	54.0	103.7
Workshops	135	10462	55.6	54.4
Exhibitions	25	32673	41.9	64.5
Free Lectures	6	1104	41.8	44.8

III. Strong advancement in cultural heritage protection

1. Taking care of cultural heritage

In 2023, the Ministry of Culture and Tourism, in partnership with the National Cultural Heritage Administration continued to advance the project aimed at tracing the origins of Chinese civilization and the "Archaeology of China" initiative. Substantial breakthroughs in underwater archaeology were made, China's deep-sea archaeological research were improved and reached world-leading standards, and archaeology in border areas also received significant attention and reinforcement. The fourth comprehensive national survey of cultural heritage was launched, preservation and development of national parks based on archaeological sites were strengthened. Efforts were also made to enhance the conservation and utilization of cultural heritage related to the Grand Canal and the Yangtze River, as well as the preservation of bridge-towers, wall paintings, clay sculptures, and relics of Northeast United Resistance Army. The management of revolutionary cultural heritage were prioritized, leading to continuous improvement in their conservation and utilization levels.The Cultural Landscape of Old Tea Forests of Jingmai Mountain in Pu'er was inscribed onto the UNESCO World Heritage list. The Ministry also ramped up its efforts to combat violations of cultural heritage laws, intensifying inspections, warnings, and enforcement actions, while launching a sustained campaign to prevent and fight cultural heritage crimes. The Guidelines on Enhancing Cultural-Heritage-related Technology Innovation was issued, alongside the organization of a national vocational skills competition in the cultural heritage sector. These initiatives reflect the Ministry's ongoing commitment to fostering innovation and talent development in the field of cultural heritage preservation. The Ministry also strengthened the authorization and management of national cultural heritage protection and management model zones, and organized more theme exhibitions related to revolutionary cultural heritage. International Museum Day and Cultural and Natural Heritage Day were celebrated with public awareness-raising programs, and documentaries such as "The Origins of China" and "The Making of Zhongguo" were co-produced, fostering a greater appreciation for China's rich cultural heritage among the audience. The opening of new museum halls, including those in the Sichuan Sanxingdui Museum and the Zhijiang Hall of Zhejiang Museum, along with major exhibitions like "A New Era of Archaeological Achievements" sparked renewed interest in museums. The Ministry also deepened and expanded international exchanges and cooperation in the field of cultural heritage, and initiated the founding of The Alliance for Cultural Heritage in Asia (ACHA). The projects to protect ancient books and train talents in this area were implemented, and the guidelines for identifying and classify ancient books were formulated. The protection of shuishu writing system and oracle bones was strengthened, and a re-examination of key ancient book protection institutions was organized. The Ministry also promoted the digitization of ancient books and the development of a digital service platform for ancient books, making the management of ancient books more scientific and standardized.

By the end of the year, there were 9,645 cultural heritage institutions all over China.-The number of employees by cultural heritage institutions reached 181,000. Among them, 13,000 were with senior professional titles, accounting for 7.0%; and 24,000 were with medium-grade professional titles, accounting for 13.1%. The number of registered museums and memorial halls nationwide has reached 6833.

By the end of 2023, there were 50.172 million cultural relics (or sets of artifacts) in the collections of the cultural heritage institutions. Among these, the amount of items (sets) in museums managed by heritage authorities totaled to 33.633 million, which accounted for 67.0% of the total.

In 2023, a total of 30,000 exhibitions were held by various cultural heritage institutions across the country. Among these, 13,000 were permanent exhibitions[12] and 17,000 were temporary exhibitions[13]. The total number of visitors reached 1,402,660,000, an increase of 119.3% compared to the previous year. Among the visitors, 322,030,000 were minors, an increase of 101.2%, accounting for 23.0% of all visitors. The state-owned museums managed by the cultural heritage system received 1,021,290,000 visitors, an increase of 123.7%, accounting for 72.8% of the total number of visitors received by cultural heritage institutions.

Figure 4: Person-time of audiences and minors cultural relic agencies accepting in 2013-2023

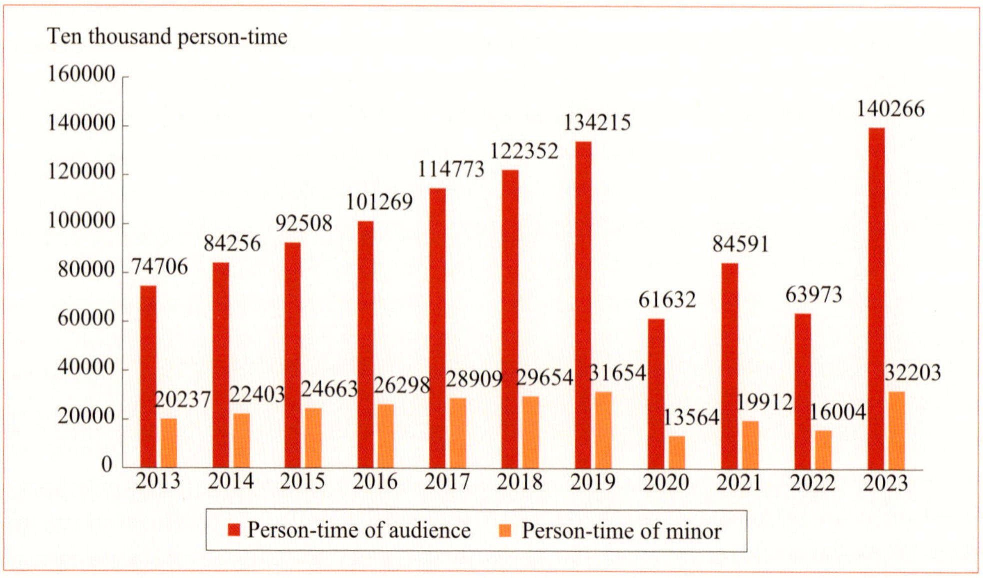

2. Intangible cultural heritage (ICH) safeguarding

In 2023, the Ministry of Culture and Tourism made significant strides in the promotion and protection of Intangible Cultural Heritage (ICH), diligently advancing the identification of the sixth batch of national-level ICH bearers, thereby steadily augmenting the ranks of these esteemed custodians of cultural traditions. The Ministry launched the Yellow River Basin and the Great Canal ICH Protection Action Plan, and carried out a comprehensive assessment of the viability of traditional crafts. Furthermore, the Ministry harnessed ICH for rural revitalization, an initiative that has seen the establishment of over 6,700 ICH workshops across the country. The China ICH Bear Research and Training Program was implemented. This initiative involved adjustments to the list of 130 participating training institutions. Ten national cultural ecological reserves were designated. The list of 100 national ICH production-based protection demonstration bases was published for public supervision. The Ministry also facilitated the deep integration of ICH with tourism, and hosted a series of events such as the China Chengdu International ICH Festival, the China Folk Song Festival, convention of ICH brands, ICH shopping fairs, and the TV programs to showcase ICH and customs in various localities of China. The Ministry organized over 12,000 ICH transmission activities related to the Chinese New Year, and over 9,800 ICH awareness raising activities on cultural and natural heritage day. The television program "China in the ICH" was produced, with over 7.54 billion views and interactions, a testament to the program's success in expanding the reach of ICH.

By the end of 2023, there were 2,241 national-level representative intangible cultural heritage (ICH) bearers recognized by the Ministry of Culture and Tourism who were still alive and 1,557 national-level representative ICH elements endorsed by the State Council. There were 43 Chinese elements inscribed on the UNESCO Representative List of the Intangible Cultural Heritage of Humanity.

By the end of 2023, there were a total of 2,406 ICH safeguarding institutions across the country, with 17,000 employees. Throughout the year in the country, these institutions held 82,000 showcases, up by 41.5%, 18,000 folklore activities, up by 30.4%, and 22,000 exhibitions, up by 20.1%.

IV. Better management for market development

In 2023, the Ministry of Culture and Tourism actively propelled the implementation of policies designed to foster steady growth and offer relief to struggling cultural and tourism enterprises. The Ministry also promoted the application of electronic certificates for cultural and tourism businesses, developing a service APP that streamlined administrative processes and provided "one-stop service". We strengthened regulation of large-scale for-profit shows, and reinforced the content supervision of stand-up comedy shows and Karaoke music tracks. The Ministry advanced the development of a market credit system for the culture and tourism sectors, and conducted pilot projects of responsible tourism and credit economy. National vocational contests for employees of star hotels and tour guides were organized to encourage capacity building within the cultural and tourism sectors.

In 2023, the Ministry guided all 31 provinces and equivalent administrative units to issue provincial-level guidance directories for comprehensive law enforcement in the cultural market. The Ministry strengthened the law enforcement supervision of large-scale for-profit performances, guiding local authorities to establish and improve long-term mechanisms for the regulation of such performances. The Ministry conducted a special action plan to regulate the box office of for-profit shows, taking stringent measures to punish any illegal acts and regulation violation in selling tickets. The Ministry continued its efforts to keep the tourism market in order, imposing penalties on travel businesses without proper certificates and those that organized hoax low-priced tours. In collaboration with the Department of Copyright Management of the Publicity Department of the CPC Central Committee, the Ministry issued a notification to further strengthen the protection of copyright owned by minors, as part of a broader effort to safeguard minors. The Ministry also promoted the development and wide use of the national cultural market technical supervision and service platform, continuously upgrading and optimizing the platform's integrated law enforcement system. Enhancing dynamic monitoring of the internet, the Ministry processed 970,000 leads of problematic issues, and handled 390,000 reports and complaints.

By the end of the year, business units in the nationwide cultural market[14] reached 175,000, according to data submitted by these units, with 1,177,000 employees and a revenue of 1,785.25 billion yuan. The profit was 138.71 billion yuan.

Among them, there were 45,000 entertainment venues with 418,000 employees, generating 58.96 billion yuan in revenue and 3.95 billion yuan in profit. There were 90,000 internet cafes with 147,000 employees, generating 18.18 billion yuan in revenue. The performing arts market had 24,000 units with 423,000 employees, generating 705.78 billion yuan in revenue and 28.39 billion yuan in profit. There were 7,000 art dealers with 22,000 employees, generating 56.38 billion yuan in revenue and 13.78 billion yuan in profit. Business units engaged in internet cultural operations totaled 8,000, with 167,000 employees, generating 945.95 billion yuan in revenue and 87.77 billion yuan in profit.

V. Further developments in cultural industry and related technology

In 2023, the Ministry of Culture and Tourism diligently continued its efforts to stimulate consumption in the cultural and tourism sectors, executed the program to stimulate spending on culture and tourism in a hundred cities and districts for the benefit of business growth and the increase of people's income. This was complemented by the issuance of the guideline for the development of hubs for national nighttime cultural and tourism consumption. The Ministry also promoted the development of national cultural and tourism consumption model cities and pilot cities, as well as national-level nighttime cultural and tourism consumption hubs.To support rural revitalization, the Ministry initiated pilot projects for cultural industries to empower rural communities, announcing the first batch of 63 pilot regions. The Ministry also advanced the growth of regional cultural industry belts, strengthening the management of national demonstration zones (bases) for cultural industries. The Ministry organized the cultural and tourism trade promotion activities under the banner of celebrating China's diversified local products and festivities. The Ministry introduced a series of policies and measures to support high-quality development in rural tourism and to enhance the management of tourist destinations during the summer vacation. The Ministry hosted a national conference on cultural and tourism project development and financing, during which strategic cooperation agreements were signed with the China Import and Export Bank and the China Agricultural Bank. The Ministry improved the coordination mechanism for cultural and tourism industry projects, promoting the implementation of the government's loan policy for facility upgrades in the cultural and tourism sectors. It also published the first two national demonstration zones for cooperation between culture and finance.The Ministry encouraged the efforts to make use of real estate investment trusts (REITs) in cultural and tourism infrastructure development, a move that included the tourism sector in the new government-private partnership (PPP) mechanism. The list of 50 national demonstration zones for the integration of cultural industries and tourism was published. "One Troupe, One Production" project for state-owned performing arts groups to produce digital shows was implemented. The Ministry also released the national list of outstanding art shows in tourist destinations, and organized a national performing arts expo.

According to the National Bureau of Statistics, in 2023, the total turnover of major cultural and culture related businesses reached 12951.5 billion yuan, increasing by 8.2% over that of the previous year.

In 2023, the Ministry of Culture and Tourism steadfastly advanced the implementation of the national strategy of digitizing cultural properties. Collaborating with the Cyberspace Administration of China, the Ministry co-hosted the sub-forum on digital culture under the Sixth Digital China Summit, publishing 44 cases of innovative digitalization of contents in the area of culture and tourism in 2023. To promote the efforts to use science and technology to power innovation, the Ministry recommended two R&D projects to be included onto the list of national-level key projects, released the names of 18 innovative R&D projects for culture and tourism and projects from the Ministry's key laboratories, gave authorization to 8 new role model parks for tourism-related technology, , and established 12 more technology innovation centers under the Ministry's auspices. To enhance standard operations in the cultural and tourism sectors, the Ministry issued the management measures for ensuring standardization of work in the field of culture and tourism. The Ministry also facilitated the release of 5 national standards, approved and issued 15 industry standards, proposed 28 standards to be established, and made efforts to establish two international standards. The scope of these standards covered a wide range of areas, including tourism, theaters, libraries, cultural centers, intangible cultural heritage, cultural contents on the internet, and cartoon and animation. They encompassed evaluations of rural tourism and smart tourism, as well as service requirements for tourist attractions, hotels, new spaces for performing arts, and online performances, and technical specifications for performance equipment and cartoon and animation platforms. These efforts collectively improved the levels of management and services, laying a solid foundation for high-quality development of the cultural and tourism industries. Furthermore, the Ministry made significant strides in the development of the three major systems of Chinese art studies, initiating 251 projects supported by national social sciences fund, 53 ministerial-level research projects and 42 projects for young talents. The Ministry also took the lead in drafting standards and guidelines to regulate study tours. 39 projects to improve vocational education in culture, arts and tourism across the country were implemented.

VI. Steady growth seen in tourism

In 2023, the Ministry of Culture and Tourism has executed Several Measures to Unlock Tourism Consumption Potential and Promote High-Quality Development of Tourism" and issued the Domestic Tourism Development Plan (2023-2025) to further tap into tourism's economic potential and elevate the industry to new heights. The Ministry has also released the "northeast region tourism development plan" and promoted the implementation of the plan to protect and transmit cultural heritage related to Yangtze and Yellow Rivers, as well as the comprehensive development strategy for culture and tourism along the Grand Canal. The Ministry Actively engaged in policy planning for the Yangtze River Economic Belt's development, the Beijing-Tianjin-Hebei region's integrated growth, the rise of the central region, and the full revitalization of northeast China. The plan for Yangtze River national cultural park development and protection was drafted, and efforts were made to bolster the creation of cultural icons that represented Chinese culture and support the construction of key sections within the Great Wall national cultural park. The Ministry is implementing a tourism program designed to foster ethnic exchanges and cultural bond, thus strengthening the shared sense of identity among the Chinese nation. This year, 18 new national-level tourist resorts, 110 tourism and leisure blocks, 7 ski resorts, 13 national sports tourism demonstration bases, and 69 industrial tourism demonstration bases. The first list of pilot spaces for immersive smart tourism experiences and "5G + smart tourism" pilot programs was published. Efforts were made to improve the quality of rural tourism by releasing premium travel routes. The Ministry carried out the project to enrich the soul and educate the youth through tourism in destinations significant in early CPC history, and hosted the 4th national contest for tour guides specialized in tourism related to early CPC history, as well as the 14th tour package design contest for college students regarding to tourism related to early CPC history. The Ministry has organized promotion activities including “tourism for a better life” nationwide showcases of various destinations, and the ice and snow tourism season. China Yiwu Cultural Products Trade Fair, the

China (Wuhan) Culture and Tourism Expo, and the China Tourism Industry Expo have been held, further increasing the publicity of cultural and tourism industries of different localities.

By the end of 2023, travel agencies across the country reached 56,275. According to the statistics of the travel agency database, their total sales in 2023 reached 444.27 billion yuan, with a profit of 3.74 billion yuan.

By the end of the year, there were in total 8,253 star hotels in China. Among them, the statistics of 7,337 were checked by cultural and tourism administrations. According to the statistics they report, their total sales in 2023 reached 160.9 billion yuan, with the average daily rate (ADR) of 370.8 yuan room/night and the average occupancy rate of 50.7%.

By the end of this year, there were 15,721 A-level tourist sites in China, with 1.607 million employees. Their total revenue in 2023 reached 406.87 billion yuan, with total visits of 5.75 billion.

Throughout the year, 4.89 billion domestic visits were made by Chinese tourists, an increase of 93.3% year-on-year. Among these, urban residents made 3.76 billion domestic trips, up by 94.9%, and rural residents made 1.13 billion domestic trips, up by 88.5%. Total spending by domestic tourists amounted to 4.9 trillion yuan, up by 140.3%. Of this, urban residents spent 4.2 trillion yuan, up by 147.5% year-on-year, and rural residents, 0.7 trillion yuan, up by 106.4%.

Figure 5: Domestic tourism development in 2013-2023

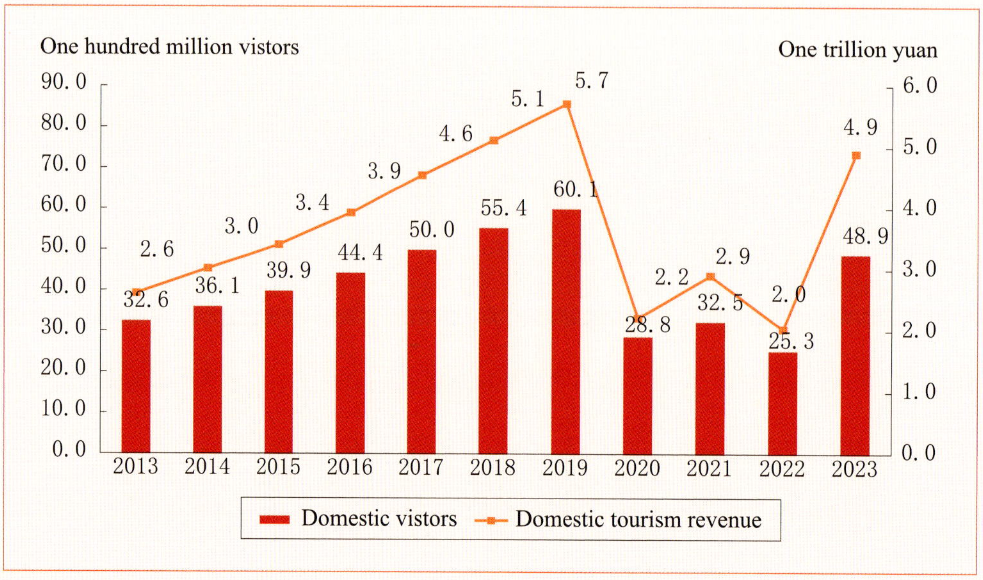

In 2023, China received 82.03 million inbound visits, among which 13.78 million were made by foreigners, and 68.24 million by compatriots from Hong Kong, Macao, and Taiwan. Meanwhile, 87.63 million outbound trips were made by residents from the Chinese mainland.

VII. Further achievements in international cultural and tourism exchange and bonding with Hong Kong, Macao and Taiwan

In 2023, the Ministry of Culture and Tourism has carried out the inbound tourism promotion plan. It has taken the lead in the organization of the gala shows of the China-Central Asia Summit and the 3rd Belt and Road Forum for International Cooperation. The Ministry also successfully held the China-Spain Year of Culture and Tourism, “Silk Road: Artists’ Rendezvous” painting exhibition and dialogue between Chinese and Arab artists, the "Echoes of Ancient Tang Poems" concert, and the concert marking the 50th anniversary of the Philadelphia Orchestra's visit to China. The "Hello! China" national tourism brand promotion campaign has been launched. The "Cultural Silk Road" initiative was carried out, and the Silk Road alliances mechanism was improved. The Ministry also held a series of events, including the "Happy Chinese New Year", "Tea for Harmony", "A Mooment to Share: Mid-Autumn Festival" global celebration, "China Stories" lecture series, "Discover China" tours, China International Travel Mart, and the Silk Road (Dunhuang) International Cultural Expo. The establishment of the International Tourism Alliance of Silk Road Cities has further strengthened the Ministry's efforts in promoting Chinese culture to a global audience. Efforts have been made to strengthen overseas platforms such as China Cultural Centers and Overseas Tourism Offices. The Ministry has also been dedicated to deepening cultural and tourism exchanges with Hong Kong, Macao, and Taiwan, organizing the 2024 Conference of China Study Tour Union for Teenagers from Hong Kong and Macao to foster extensive interaction and in-depth exchanges between the youths from Chinese mainland and those from Hong Kong and Macao. Efforts have been made to reinforce Macao's position as a base for cultural exchanges, with a focus on Chinese culture as the mainstream and celebrating the coexistence of diverse cultures. The cross-straits tour operators' conference has been held, offering a wide range of opportunities for deepening tourism cooperation across the Taiwan Strait.

By the end of the year, there were in total 48 overseas China Cultural Centers and 20 Chinese tourism offices in foreign countries. Moreover, we also have established the Asia Tourism Exchange Center in Hong Kong, and the offices of Association For Tourism Exchange Across The Taiwan Straits in Taipei and Gaoxiong.

VIII. Stronger support from the central budget

The total amount of cultural and tourism undertaking expenses[15] for the whole year was 128.04 billion yuan, an increase of 7.86 billion yuan over that of the previous year, up by 6.5%; as for the national cultural and tourism undertaking expenses per capita, the total was 90.8 yuan, an increase of 5.7 yuan over the previous year, up by 6.7%. Cultural and tourism undertaking expenses accounted for 0.47% of the state expenditure of China, an increase of 0.01 percentage points from the previous year.

Figure 6: National cultural and tourism undertaking expenses per capita (2013-2023)

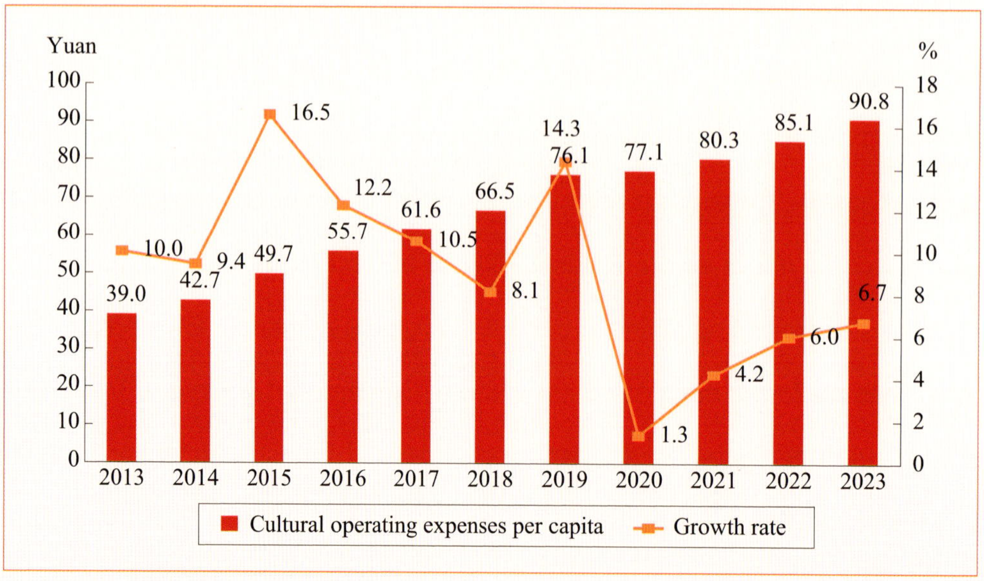

Regarding the national cultural and tourism undertaking expenses, that of cultural and tourism units above county level was 59.76 billion yuan, accounting for 46.7%, 1.5 percentage points higher than that of the previous year; that of cultural and tourism units of county level or below the level of county was 68.27 billion yuan, accounting for 53.3%, down by 1.5 percentage points in the sense of its proportion. The cultural and tourism undertaking expenses of the eastern region[16] reached

56.00 billion yuan, accounting for 43.7%, and its proportion decreased by 1.4 percentage points; that of the central region reached 32.41 billion yuan, accounting for 25.3%, its proportion increased by 0.1 percentage points; and that of the western region reached 36.74 billion yuan, accounting for 28.7%, 1.4 percentage points higher than the number of the previous year.

Table 2: Urban & Rural and Regional-based distribution of national cultural undertaking expenses

		In 2000	In 2005	In 2010	In 2015	In 2020	In 2022	In 2023
Aggregate (one hundred million yuan)	**Nationwide**	**63.2**	**133.8**	**323.1**	**686.0**	**1088.3**	**1201.8**	**1280.4**
	# Above county level	46.3	98.1	206.7	352.8	501.0	544.3	597.6
	County level and below level of county	16.9	35.7	116.4	330.1	587.3	658.6	682.7
	# Eastern region	28.9	64.4	143.4	287.9	491.6	542.5	560.0
	Central region	15.1	30.6	78.7	164.3	269.8	302.6	324.1
	Western region	13.7	27.6	85.8	193.9	301.6	328.1	367.4
Proportion (%)	**Nationwide**	**100.0**	**100.0**	**100.0**	**100.0**	**100.0**	**100.0**	**100.0**
	# Above county level	73.4	73.3	64.0	51.7	46.0	45.2	46.7
	County level and below level of county	26.7	26.7	36.0	48.3	54.0	54.8	53.3
	# Eastern region	45.7	48.1	44.4	42.1	45.1	45.1	43.7
	Central region	23.8	22.9	24.3	24.1	24.8	25.2	25.3
	Western region	21.7	20.6	26.6	28.4	27.7	27.3	28.7

Notes:

[1] All the data of the communiqué are preliminary statistical data. Statistics of Hong Kong SAR, Macao SAR, and Taiwan are not included. Some of data are not compatible with the total of

sub-entries due to rounding off.

[2] Cultural and tourism units refer to cultural institutions or business units that cultural and tourism administrations of all levels across the country organize or manage as related institutions in the cultural and tourism fields, excluding institutions organized or managed by authorities of press and publications, radio , film and television, etc. According to the current statistical system, the cultural institutions (such as public libraries, cultural centers, cultural stations, museums, state-owned art performance troupes and performing arts venues, etc.) organized by cultural authorities are all brought into the statistical range. Regarding business units managed as related institutions in the cultural and tourism fields, including private art performance troupes, for-profit venues, cybercafés, art dealers, show business agencies, Level-A tourist destinations, star hotels and travel agencies, related statistics are all included.

[3] The employees refer to the people who work with and receive payment from cultural and tourism administrations of all levels across the country organize or manage as related institutions in the cultural and tourism fields.

[4] The art performance troupes mean various professional artistic performance organizations organized by cultural institutions or to which the cultural and tourism administrations organize or manage as related institutions in the cultural and tourism fields (authorized by cultural and tourism authorities and with commercial performance license), and is engaged in such activities as performing arts, as well as professional private troupes (amateur part-time groups not included).

[5] An art museum refers to a state-owned art museum that cultural and tourism administrations organize or manage as related institutions in the cultural and tourism fields, with functions such as exhibitions, collections, research, public education, and other services, and is open to the public. It also refers to a non-profit private art museum that is registered with the civil affairs authorities and acknowledged by the cultural and tourism administrations with similar functions as above.

[6] Public libraries refer to libraries organized by cultural and tourism administrations for public use.

[7] The total number of books collected in public libraries refers to the sum of ancient books,

books, collections of periodicals and newspapers, and manuals and manuscripts in the libraries' catalogues, as well as audiovisual materials including micro-reproductions, videotapes, audio tapes and CDs.

[8] The total flow of person-time of public library refers to the gross visits made by the people to enjoy the services of the libraries in that year, including borrowing books, making inquiries and participating in readers' activities.

[9] The cultural institutions for mass public and communities refer to the places that cultural and tourism authorities at all levels organize for mass cultural activities, mainly including cultural centers (including comprehensive cultural centers and public art centers) and cultural stations.

[10] The number of activities means the sum of the activities including cultural, literary and artistic events, training classes, exhibitions, and public lectures.

[11] The cultural and arts groups refer to art groups composed by the staff members of the above-mentioned institutions that present non-profit art performances.

[12] A permanent exhibitions refers to an exhibition in the museum at a fixed location which runs a long time.

[13] A temporary exhibition means an exhibition curated and installed by the museum, often varying in forms.

[14] Business units of cultural markets refer to the companies approved or acknowledged and have relevant licenses and filing documents, and that engage in cultural businesses and services. In line with the current statistical systems, the statistical range of business units of the cultural market include for-profit show business venues, internet cafés, for-profit private art performance troupes, internet companies specialized in culture, art dealing companies and show business agencies.

[15] Cultural and tourism undertaking expense means aggregate of expenditures that the budget of all levels in the area invests to the cultural and tourism administrations. According to current statistical caliber, cultural operating expense does not include administrative expenditures of cultural and tourism administration and management departments at all levels.

[16] The Eastern region includes Beijing, Tianjin, Liaoning Province, Shanghai, Jiangsu

Province, Fujian Province, Shandong Province, and Guangdong Province; Central region includes Hebei Province, Shanxi Province, Jilin Province, Heilongjiang Province, Anhui Province, Jiangxi Province, Henan Province, Hubei Province, Hunan Province and Hainan Province; Western region includes Inner Mongolia (autonomous region), Guangxi (autonomous region), Chongqing, Sichuan Province, Guizhou Province, Yunan Province, Xizang (autonomous region), Shannxi Province, Gansu Province, Qinghai Province, Ningxia (autonomous region), and Xinjiang (autonomous region).